W9-ARV-486

HOW
ELECTIONS
WORK

BY JEANNE MARIE FORD

childsworld.com

Published by The Child's World®
1980 Lookout Drive • Mankato, MN 56003-1705
800-599-READ • www.childsworld.com

ACKNOWLEDGMENTS
The Child's World®: Mary Swensen, Publishing Director
Red Line Editorial: Editorial direction and production
The Design Lab: Design

Photographs ©: Hill Street Studios/Blend Images/Corbis, cover, 2;
Shutterstock Images, 5, 19; Bettmann/Corbis, 6, 13; iStockphoto,
10, 17; Georgios Kollidas/Shutterstock Images, 12; Jim Mone/
AP Images, 15; John Amis/EPA/Corbis, 20; Chris Keane/Reuters/
Corbis, 21

ISBN 9781503809024
LCCN 2015958456

Printed in the United States of America
PA02354

**On the cover: Americans vote at a polling place
on Election Day.**

TABLE OF CONTENTS

CHAPTER 1

VOTING RIGHTS

Voting has always been important to Americans. In 1776, the United States declared independence. Part of the reason was people's desire to vote. Colonists wanted a say in the laws. But they were ruled by the British. The American colonists had no government **representatives**. Britain and the rebel colonists went to war. In 1783, the war ended. Britain surrendered. Americans began to set up a new government. Finally, they could vote for their leaders.

In 1787, the nation's founders wrote the Constitution. It is the law of the land. The Constitution said the United States was a **democracy**. The nation would be governed by and for the people. The Constitution promised many rights. The right to vote was mentioned most often. However, the Constitution did not give every citizen the right to vote.

The founders debated who should be able to vote. The Constitution left many voting laws to the states. At first,

Since 1800, the U.S. Congress has met in the Capitol building. Voters elect Congress members every two years.

states did not give women the right to vote or run for office. Many other groups could not vote. Thousands of slaves lived in the United States. They were denied many rights, including the right to vote. Laws also forbade free black men from voting. Native Americans did not have voting rights, either.

**Starting in 1920, women around the country
could vote in elections.**

Most states limited voting to white men with property. In the first U.S. election, 94 percent of Americans could not vote. Over time, more Americans won the right to vote. **Amendments** changed the Constitution. After the Civil War, slavery was outlawed. Former slaves became U.S. citizens. In 1870, the 15th Amendment was ratified. This amendment gave black men the right to vote. Women continued to fight for **suffrage**. In 1920, the 19th Amendment gave them the right to vote.

Many people worked bravely for voting rights. They faced challenges even after the new amendments passed.

VOTING RIGHTS TIMELINE

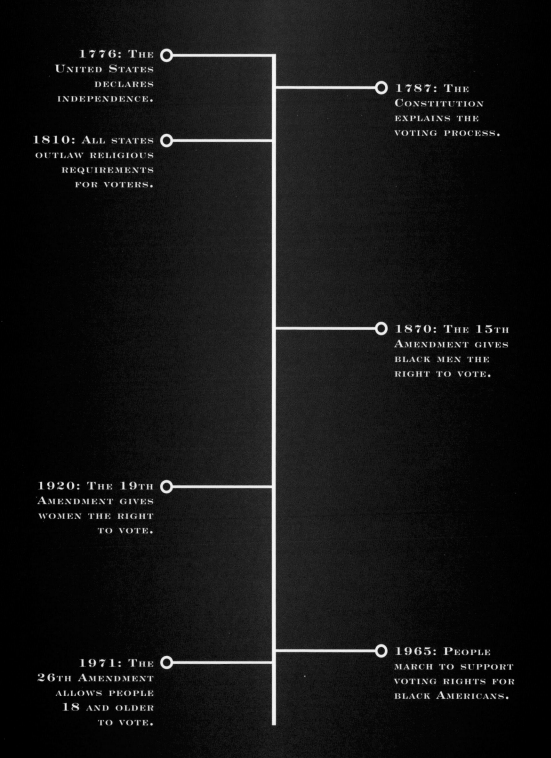

1776: THE UNITED STATES DECLARES INDEPENDENCE.

1787: THE CONSTITUTION EXPLAINS THE VOTING PROCESS.

1810: ALL STATES OUTLAW RELIGIOUS REQUIREMENTS FOR VOTERS.

1870: THE 15TH AMENDMENT GIVES BLACK MEN THE RIGHT TO VOTE.

1920: THE 19TH AMENDMENT GIVES WOMEN THE RIGHT TO VOTE.

1971: THE 26TH AMENDMENT ALLOWS PEOPLE 18 AND OLDER TO VOTE.

1965: PEOPLE MARCH TO SUPPORT VOTING RIGHTS FOR BLACK AMERICANS.

Some people did not want black Americans to vote. They tried to keep black men and women from participating in elections. Taxes and reading tests prevented many from voting.

Thousands of Americans protested these taxes and tests. In the 1950s and 1960s, Martin Luther King Jr. gave speeches and led marches. In 1965, President Lyndon B. Johnson signed the Voting Rights Act. This law made it illegal to stop people from voting. In 1971, another important voting measure passed. The 26th Amendment lowered the voting age from 21 to 18.

Americans have always valued the right to vote. Elections make sure that people can choose their leaders. "One person, one vote" is an American value. Each vote should count the same as every other. Every citizen should have an equal say.

VOTING REQUIREMENTS

Some national laws control who can vote. American voters must be at least 18 years old. Voters must live in the district where they plan to vote. States also have voting laws. Some stop people found guilty of crimes from voting. Many also require voters to show identification.

CHAPTER 2

THE VOTING PROCESS

Voting gives people a voice in decisions that affect them. People vote for the mayor of their town or city. They choose state leaders, including governors. They elect members of Congress. And they vote for the U.S. president. These elections can be complicated. Election **campaigns** last for months or even years.

Political **candidates** try to persuade people to vote for them. They give speeches. They meet with voters. They participate in debates. Candidates talk about their views. Often, they use advertisements.

Most candidates run as part of a political party. Parties are groups of people with similar ideas. The United States has two main parties: the Democratic Party and the Republican Party. Many Republicans want a limited role for government. They also believe in low taxes. Republicans often support business owners. They believe that businesses can help the economy. Many Democrats believe in a larger

In 2012, President Barack Obama spoke to a crowd in Virginia. That year, Obama was reelected president.

role for the **federal** government. They think government programs aid people in need. Democrats usually oppose giving more power to large businesses. However, not all Democrats or Republicans are the same. The beliefs of the parties have changed over time.

In most elections, one person runs from each party. Candidates may also run from smaller parties. But parties were not always part of U.S. politics. George Washington was the first president. He had no political party. Washington warned against making parties powerful. He said they would divide people. Yet parties soon formed anyway. The parties brought together people with similar views. They provided money and resources. Parties helped candidates get elected.

Parties play a major role in primary elections. These occur before the general or main elections. In primaries, voters select candidates to run for a party. There are Democratic and Republican primaries. A few states also hold **caucuses**. Officials announce the winner of a primary or caucus. The winner runs against a candidate from the other party in the general election. All states have a presidential primary or

U.S. POLITICAL PARTIES

The United States has had many parties. The first was the Federalists. This party was formed in the 1700s. Federalists supported a strong central government. Another party was the Democratic-Republicans. They wanted more rights for the states. Many political parties have come and gone. The Republicans and Democrats have been the major parties since the 1860s.

George Washington, the first president, did not
have a political party.

At a Republican Party convention in 1880,
delegates gathered to choose a candidate.

caucus. The person with the most total votes becomes the
party **nominee**.

On Election Day, voters go to their polling places. They
may also vote by mail. Each voter receives a **ballot**. The
ballot lists the candidates. Voters mark their choices. They
can also write in the names of candidates who aren't listed.
Sometimes, ballots also include other questions. People can

vote on issues in their communities. Election officials gather the ballots. They send the ballots to a government office. Then the votes are counted.

A democracy needs fair elections. Officials try to prevent voter **fraud**. In the past, some candidates bought people's votes. Early Americans voted publicly. They stomped their feet or said "yay" or "nay." Everyone knew how others had voted. Often, groups pressured people to vote a certain way. Bribes made elections unfair.

Methods of voting have changed over time. By the 1850s, people used paper ballots. These ballots were secret. They helped make voting private. Secret ballots helped prevent bribes and threats. However, voters sometimes made errors. Their votes were not marked clearly. Now many polling places have electronic voting machines. People vote privately in booths. They can review their choices. Vote counting today is fairer than it used to be. Voting machines are often more accurate than paper ballots. But officials can still make mistakes. In close elections, officials count the ballots twice to prevent errors. They check each ballot carefully. Reporters announce the election winners.

Minnesota held a close election for governor in 2010. Workers recounted all of the ballots to make sure the results were correct.

When politicians win elections, they serve their **terms**. Then they can run for reelection. Sometimes, people disagree with how officials do their jobs. When this happens, they can call for special elections. A **recall** election ends a politician's term early. People then vote for a new candidate. However, this kind of election is rare.

Voting is both a right and a duty. Voters take part in key decisions. Informed voters make sure they choose wisely. They can help good candidates win.

CHAPTER 3

NATIONAL ELECTIONS

The U.S. government has three branches. The legislative branch includes the U.S. Congress. This branch makes laws. The executive branch enforces laws. This branch is led by the president. The judicial branch is our court system.

Voters elect the president. They also elect members of Congress. Some local judges are elected. People do not vote for federal judges. The president chooses these judges.

Congress has two houses. One is the House of Representatives. It has 435 members. The number of House members is based on how many people live in each state. The other house is the Senate. The Senate has 100 members. Each state has two senators. House members serve a term of two years. Senate terms are for six years. Presidents serve for four. Members of Congress can be elected many times. However, the president can serve only two terms.

**Voters choose nominees for president and
vice president as a team.**

The Constitution lists requirements for politicians. The president and vice president must be at least 35 years old. They must be born in the United States. Candidates for Congress must live in the states they will represent. A Senate candidate must be at least 30 years old. A House candidate must be at least 25.

In presidential elections, each nominee chooses a running mate. The running mate is a candidate for vice president.

If the president cannot do the job, the vice president takes over. The vice president is also president of the Senate.

Primaries are usually held early in the year. Then both parties hold conventions. These are large gatherings of party members. At the conventions, members officially select the nominees. A presidential election takes place every four years. People vote on a Tuesday in early November. The new president takes office in January.

Americans do not vote for the president directly. They vote for people called electors, who promise to vote for certain candidates. This system is called the Electoral College. The electors vote for the president.

Our nation's founders began the Electoral College. They created the system for a few reasons. One was that it balanced power among all states. There are 538 electors. States have one elector for each member of

VOTER TURNOUT

Not everyone votes on Election Day. In some elections, only 40 percent of voters vote. Voter turnout is highest in presidential elections. Then, it is usually about 60 percent. U.S. voter turnout is low compared to some other countries. However, many people are determined to vote. In some elections, voters wait for hours to cast their ballots.

2012 PRESIDENTIAL ELECTION RESULTS MAP

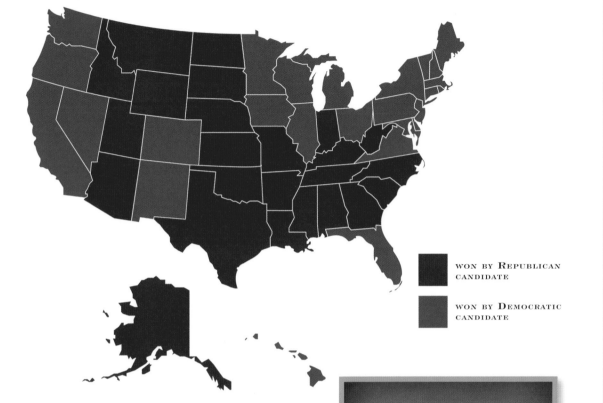

WON BY REPUBLICAN CANDIDATE

WON BY DEMOCRATIC CANDIDATE

This map shows the results from the 2012 presidential election. The Democratic candidate, Barack Obama, ran against Republican Mitt Romney. Obama won 26 states and 332 electoral votes. Romney won 24 states and 206 electoral votes.

Congress. There are also three electors from Washington, DC. Winning the election takes at least 270 electoral votes. As a result, candidates need to appeal to people from all regions. They need enough electoral votes from different parts of the country.

Most states use a "winner take all" system. The most popular candidate in the state wins all of the state's electoral

New York voters lined up to vote in
the 2014 congressional election.

votes. In other states, candidates can divide the electoral
votes. Usually, the person with the most **popular votes**
nationwide wins the race. But sometimes the candidate
with the most popular votes does not win the electoral
vote. Another candidate wins the electoral vote and
becomes president.

Some say the electoral system is unfair. They support a
direct popular vote. However, changing the system would
be difficult. It would require changing the Constitution.

An election judge taps in a code on a voting machine. Many people vote electronically.

For now, the U.S. electoral system is here to stay. People have many ways to get involved in the political process. They can volunteer on campaigns or at polling places. They can run for office. Simplest of all, they can make their voices heard by voting.

amendments (uh-MEND-munts) Amendments are additions or changes to documents. Amendments to the Constitution guarantee Americans many freedoms.

ballot (BAL-ut) A ballot is the list of candidates in an election. Voters mark their choices on a ballot.

campaigns (kam-PEYNZ) Campaigns are efforts to persuade people to vote for a certain candidate. Speeches and advertisements are often part of campaigns.

candidates (KAN-di-deytz) Candidates are people who run for office. Candidates for president must be at least 35 years old.

caucuses (KAW-kus-iz) Caucuses are gatherings of voters from a particular party. At caucuses, the voters select the person they want to run in the general election.

democracy (di-MOK-ruh-see) A democracy is a government run by the people. The United States is a democracy.

federal (FED-er-ul) The federal government is the national government. The president is the head of the federal government.

fraud (FRAWD) Fraud is trickery or lies. Voter fraud could include a voter pretending to be someone else.

nominee (nom-uh-NEE) A nominee is a person who is chosen to run for office. At party conventions, members officially select the nominee.

popular votes (POP-yuh-ler VOTES) Popular votes are votes from the American people. Popular votes are different from electoral votes, which are votes from members of the Electoral College.

recall (REE-kawl) A recall election allows voters to remove a politician from office. A state or community might hold a recall election.

representatives (rep-ri-ZEN-tuh-tivz) Representatives are people who can represent or speak for others. Government representatives might support laws to help their communities.

suffrage (SUF-rij) When people have suffrage, they have the right to vote. Many people have fought for suffrage.

terms (TURMZ) Terms are periods of time that politicians serve in office. Presidents serve four-year terms.

TO LEARN MORE

IN THE LIBRARY

Goodman, Susan E., and Elwood H. Smith. *See How They Run: Campaign Dreams, Election Schemes, and the Race to the White House.* New York: Bloomsbury, 2012.

Jackson, Carolyn. *The Election Book: The People Pick a President.* New York: Scholastic, 2012.

Sobel, Syl. *Presidential Elections and Other Cool Facts.* Hauppauge, NY: Barron's, 2012.

ON THE WEB

Visit our Web site for links about elections: **childsworld.com/links**

Note to Parents, Teachers, and Librarians: We routinely verify our Web links to make sure they are safe and active sites. So encourage your readers to check them out!

INDEX

ABOUT THE AUTHOR

Jeanne Marie Ford is an Emmy-winning TV scriptwriter and holds a master of fine arts degree in writing for children from Vermont College. She has written numerous children's books and articles. Ford also teaches college English. She lives in Maryland with her husband and two children.